MAGIC TIME

STUDENT BOOK

2

Kathleen Kampa

Charles Vilina

OXFORD

UNIVERSITY PRESS

OXFORD
UNIVERSITY PRESS

198 Madison Avenue
New York, NY 10016 USA

Great Clarendon Street
Oxford OX2 6DP England

Oxford New York

Auckland Cape Town Dar es Salaam Hong Kong Karachi
Kuala Lumpur Madrid Melbourne Mexico City Nairobi
New Delhi Shanghai Taipei Toronto
With offices in
Argentina Austria Brazil Chile Czech Republic France Greece
Guatemala Hungary Italy Japan South Korea Poland Portugal
Singapore Switzerland Thailand Turkey Ukraine Vietnam

OXFORD is a trademark of Oxford University Press.

ISBN-13: 978 0 19 436187 3
ISBN-10: 0 19 436187 X

Library of Congress Cataloging-in-Publication Data

Kampa, Kathleen.
    Magic time student book 2/Kathleen Kampa, Charles Vilina.
        p.cm.
    Includes index.
    ISBN 0-19-436187-X
      1. English language—Textbooks for foreign speakers.
I. Vilina, Charles.

PE1128.K2833 2001
428.2'4—dc21   2001036751

Editorial Manager: Shelagh Speers
Senior Editor: Lesley Koustaff
Editor: Paul B. Phillips
Senior Production Editor: Joseph McGasko
Design Manager: Maj-Britt Hagsted
Designer: Rae Grant
Art Buyer: Jodi Waxman
Production Manager: Shanta Persaud
Production Coordinator: Eve Wong

Musical arrangements and chant music: William Hirtz

Illustrations: Yvette Banek, Cathy Beylon, Randy Chewning/HK
Portfolio, Inc., Bill Colrus, Anthony Lewis/HK Portfolio, Inc.,
Margeaux Lucas/HK Portfolio, Inc., Tammie Lyon, Benton Mahan,
Dana Regan, Michael Reid/HK Portfolio, Inc., George Ulrich/HK
Portfolio, Inc., Jamie Smith/HK Portfolio, Inc., Viki Woodworth

Original characters developed by Amy Wummer

Cover design: Silver Editions
Cover illustrations: Cheryl Mendenhall and Jim Talbot

Printing (last digit): 10 9 8 7 6 5

Printed in Hong Kong.

*Our sincere gratitude to our editors Lesley Koustaff and Paul Phillips
for patiently directing our energies and believing in our vision for
Magic Time. Special thanks to our sons John and Christian, as well
as to our parents, for their enduring love and support. Finally, to our
many students, to whom Magic Time is dedicated, thank you for
making teaching the greatest profession in the world.*

– Kathleen Kampa and Charles Vilina

Table of Contents

Syllabus

Unit	*Title*/Topic	Word Time	Use the Words	Action Word Time	Use the Action Words	Phonics Time
1	*At the Zoo/* Animals	kangaroo gorilla penguin polar bear lion giraffe	What is it? It's a penguin.	stretch run jump swim	I can stretch. Me, too.	**a**nt **a**pple **a**lligator **b**aby **b**us **b**utterfly
2	*At the Aquarium/* Aquarium	long fast big short slow small	It's slow. It isn't fast.	look at the turtle feed the turtle touch the starfish hold the starfish	Let's feed the turtle. Okay.	**c**ake **c**ar **c**at **d**entist **d**inosaur **d**onut
3	*Occupations/* Occupations	doctor firefighter teacher pilot vet student	She's a teacher. He's a vet.	write the word erase the word help the teacher point to the teacher	Please help the teacher. Sure.	**e**lf **e**gg **e**lephant **f**armer **f**eather **f**an
	Review 1					
4	*At a Restaurant/* Food	pizza bread juice spaghetti salad rice	I want pizza.	pour the juice drink the juice cut the pizza eat the pizza	Drink the juice. All right.	**g**irl **g**oat **g**arden **h**orse **h**ouse **h**en
5	*In the Backyard/* Toys	ball kite yo-yo puzzle doll jump rope	I have a kite.	push the wagon pull the wagon make the kite fly the kite	Watch me pull the wagon. Okay.	**i**nk **i**gloo **i**nsect **j**eans **j**ar **j**acket
6	*Camping Trip/* Clothes	cap sweater shirt jacket skirt dress	She has a skirt. He has a sweater.	put on your cap take off your cap take out your sweater put away your sweater	Take out your sweater quickly.	**k**etchup **k**ey **k**ing **l**izard **l**eaf **l**emon **m**ouse **m**oon **m**onkey
	Review 2					

Unit	Title/Topic	Word Time	Use the Words	Action Word Time	Use the Action Words	Phonics Time
7	Clock Shop/ Time	one o'clock– twelve o'clock	What time is it? It's two o'clock.	pick up the clock put down the clock open the door close the door	Put down the clock slowly.	numbers nest necklace ox office octopus
8	A Week at Camp Fun/ Days of the Week	Sunday Monday Tuesday Wednesday Thursday Friday Saturday	What day is it? Today is Sunday.	plant a tree climb a tree draw a picture paint a picture	Draw a picture with me. Sure.	puppy popcorn pig queen quilt question mark
9	World Weather/ Weather	sunny hot windy cloudy cold rainy	How's the weather? It's windy.	get on the train get off the train get in the car get out of the car	Let's get off the train. All right.	rooster rainbow rabbit seal sailboat sun
	Review 3					
10	At School/ School Activities	sing songs write stories read books do jumping jacks color pictures hold hands	We read books at school.	raise your hand put down your hand talk to your friend listen to your friend	Please raise your hand. Okay.	tiger table telephone umbrella umpire upside down
11	At the Park/ Sports and Hobbies	play basketball play soccer play cards play chess play the violin play the piano	Can you play soccer? Yes, I can. No, I can't.	bounce the basketball catch the basketball kick the soccer ball throw the soccer ball	I can bounce the basketball. Great!	vase violin vest worm watermelon window
12	Annie's Birthday/ Rooms of a House	bedroom bathroom yard living room dining room kitchen	Where are you? I'm in the kitchen.	wash the dishes dry the dishes turn on the light turn off the light	Turn off the light, please. All right.	fox box six yarn yo-yo yellow zebra zipper zero
	Review 4					

Introductions

A. Listen and repeat.

B.  Listen and point below.

1. Annie

2. Ted

3. Digger

4. Dot

5. Kelly

Listen and point below. Then sing along.

6.
Pat

7.
Kumi

8.
Joe

9.
Jane

10.
Chris

Word Time

A. Listen and repeat.

1.  kangaroo
2. gorilla
3. penguin
4. polar bear
5.  lion
6.  giraffe

B. Listen and point below. Then chant. **C.** Listen and write the number.

Use the Words

A. 🎧 Listen and repeat.

B. 🎧 Listen and point below.

C. 🎧 Listen and point. Then sing along.

Action Word Time

A. 🎧 Listen and repeat.

1. stretch
2. run
3. jump
4. swim

B. 🎧 Listen and repeat.

C. 🎧 Listen and point below. **D.** 🎧 Listen and point. Then sing along.

Phonics Time

A. Make the shape of each letter.

A   a   B   b

B. 🎧 Listen and point.

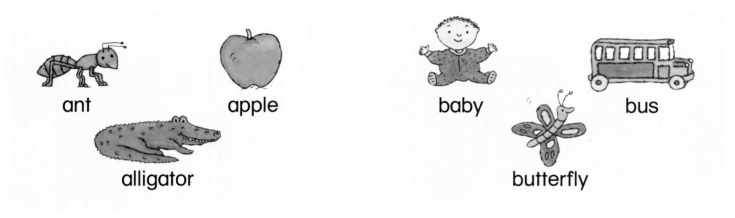

ant   apple   baby   bus

alligator   butterfly

C. 🎧 Listen and point. Then sing along.

Word Time

2

A. Listen and repeat.

1.  long

2. fast

3.  big

4. short

5. slow

6.  small

B. Listen and point below. Then chant.

C. Listen and write the number.

Use the Words

A. 🔊 Listen and repeat.

It's slow. It isn't fast.

B. 🔊 Listen and point below.

C. 🔊 Listen and point. Then sing along.

Action Word Time

A. 🎧 Listen and repeat.

1.

look at
the turtle

2.

feed
the turtle

3.

touch
the starfish

4.

hold
the starfish

B. 🎧 Listen and repeat.

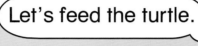

Let's feed the turtle.

Okay.

C. 🎧 Listen and point below.　　**D.** 🎧 Listen and point. Then sing along.

Phonics Time

A. Make the shape of each letter.

B. 🔊 Listen and point.

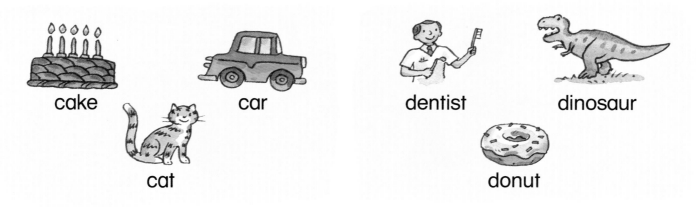

cake   car

cat

dentist   dinosaur

donut

C. 🔊 Listen and point. Then sing along.

Word Time

A. Listen and repeat.

1. doctor

2. firefighter

3. teacher

4. pilot

5.  vet

6.  student

B. Listen and point below. Then chant.

C. Listen and write the number.

Use the Words

A. Listen and repeat.

She's a teacher.

He's a vet.

B. Listen and point below.

C. Listen and point. Then sing along.

Action Word Time

A. 🎧 Listen and repeat.

1.

write
the word

2.

erase
the word

3.

help
the teacher

4.

point to
the teacher

B. 🎧 Listen and repeat.

Please write the word.

Sure.

C. 🎧 Listen and point below.

D. 🎧 Listen and point. Then sing along.

Phonics Time

A. Make the shape of each letter.

E   e   F   f

B. 🎧 Listen and point.

elf   egg   farmer   feather

elephant   fan

C. 🎧 Listen and point. Then sing along.

A. Listen and match.

1. •   2. •   3. •   4. •   5. •   6. •

B. Listen and write the number.

C. Trace the letters. Then circle and connect.

Aa   Bb   Cc   Dd   Ee   Ff

A. 📼 Listen and connect.

1. •　　　•　　•　　　•　

2. •　　　•　　•　　　•　

3. •　　　•　　•　　　•　

4. •　　　•　　•　　　•

B. 📼 Listen and write the number.

Word Time

A. Listen and repeat.

1. pizza

2. bread

3. juice

4. spaghetti

5. salad

6. rice

B. Listen and point below. Then chant.

C. Listen and write the number.

Use the Words

A. 📼 Listen and repeat.

I want pizza.

B. 📼 Listen and point below.

C. 📼 Listen and point. Then sing along.

Action Word Time

A. 🎧 Listen and repeat.

1.

pour the juice

2.

drink the juice

3.

cut the pizza

4.

eat the pizza

B. 🎧 Listen and repeat.

Drink the juice.

All right.

C. 🎧 Listen and point below.

D. 🎧 Listen and point. Then sing along.

Phonics Time

A. Make the shape of each letter.

B. 🎧 Listen and point.

girl   goat

garden

horse   house

hen

C. 🎧 Listen and point. Then sing along.

Word Time

5

A. 🎧 Listen and repeat.

1. ball
2. kite
3. yo-yo
4. puzzle
5. doll
6. jump rope

B. 🎧 Listen and point below. Then chant.

C. 🎧 Listen and write the number.

Use the Words

A. 📼 Listen and repeat.

I have a kite.

B. 📼 Listen and point below.

C. 📼 Listen and point. Then sing along.

Action Word Time

A.  Listen and repeat.

1.

push the wagon

2.

pull the wagon

3.

make the kite

4.

fly the kite

B. Listen and repeat.

C. Listen and point below.

D. Listen and point. Then sing along.

Phonics Time

A. Make the shape of each letter.

B. 🎧 Listen and point.

ink

igloo

insect

jeans

jar

jacket

C. 🎧 Listen and point. Then sing along.

Word Time

A. Listen and repeat.

1.  cap
2. sweater
3. shirt
4.  jacket
5. skirt
6. dress

B. Listen and point below. Then chant.

C. Listen and write the number.

Use the Words

A. 📼 Listen and repeat.

She has a skirt.

He has a sweater.

B. 📼 Listen and point below.

C. 📼 Listen and point. Then sing along.

Action Word Time

A. 🎧 Listen and repeat.

1.
put on
your cap

2.
take off
your cap

3.
take out
your sweater

4.
put away
your sweater

B. 🎧 Listen and repeat.

> Take out your sweater quickly.

C. 🎧 Listen and point below.

D. 🎧 Listen and point. Then sing along.

A. Make the shape of each letter.

K   k   L   I   M   m

B. 🔊 Listen and point.

ketchup   key   lizard   leaf   mouse   moon

king   lemon   monkey

C. 🔊 Listen and point. Then sing along.

A. 📼 Listen and match.

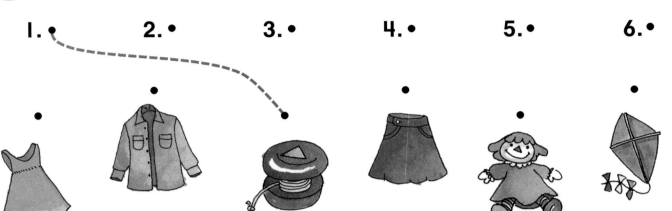

1. •   2. •   3. •   4. •   5. •   6. •

B. 📼 Listen and write the number.

C. Trace the letters. Then circle and connect.

Gg   Hh   Ii   Jj   Kk   Ll   Mm

A. 📼 Listen and connect.

1. •

•   

2. •

•   •

3. •

•   

4. •

•   •

B. 📼 Listen and write the number.

Word Time

A. 📼 Listen and repeat.

1:00	**2:00**	**3:00**	**4:00**
one o'clock	two o'clock	three o'clock	four o'clock
5:00	**6:00**	**7:00**	**8:00**
five o'clock	six o'clock	seven o'clock	eight o'clock
9:00	**10:00**	**11:00**	**12:00**
nine o'clock	ten o'clock	eleven o'clock	twelve o'clock

B. 📼 Listen and point below. Then chant.   **C.** 📼 Listen and write the number.

Use the Words

A. 🔊 Listen and repeat.

What time is it?

It's two o'clock.

B. 🔊 Listen and point below.

C. 🔊 Listen and point. Then sing along.

Action Word Time

A. 🎧 Listen and repeat.

1.

pick up
the clock

2.

put down
the clock

3.

open
the door

4.

close
the door

B. 🎧 Listen and repeat.

Put down the clock slowly.

C. 🎧 Listen and point below.

D. 🎧 Listen and point. Then sing along.

Phonics Time

A. Make the shape of each letter.

N   n   O   o

B. 🎧 Listen and point.

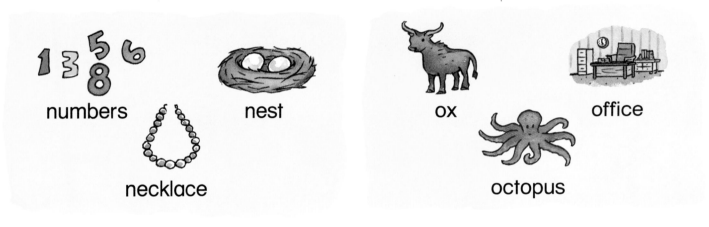

numbers   nest   ox   office

necklace   octopus

C. 🎧 Listen and point. Then sing along.

Word Time

8

A. Listen and repeat.

Sunday	Monday	Tuesday	Wednesday	Thursday	Friday	Saturday

Sunday Monday Tuesday Wednesday Thursday Friday Saturday

B. Listen and point below. Then chant.

C. Listen and write the number.

Sunday

Monday

Tuesday

Use the Words

Action Word Time

A. 📼 Listen and repeat.

1.

plant a tree

2.

climb a tree

3.

draw a picture

4.

paint a picture

B. 📼 Listen and repeat.

Draw a picture with me.

Sure.

C. 📼 Listen and point below.

D. 📼 Listen and point. Then sing along.

Phonics Time

A. Make the shape of each letter.

P   p   Q   q

B. 🎧 Listen and point.

puppy   popcorn   queen   quilt

pig   question mark

C. 🎧 Listen and point. Then sing along.

Word Time

9

A. 🎧 Listen and repeat.

1.  sunny

2. hot

3.  windy

4.  cloudy

5.  cold

6. rainy

B. 🎧 Listen and point below. Then chant.

C. 🎧 Listen and write the number.

Use the Words

A. 📼 Listen and repeat.

How's the weather?

It's windy.

B. 📼 Listen and point below.

C. 📼 Listen and point. Then sing along.

Rr

Action Word Time

A. 🔊 Listen and repeat.

1.

get on
the train

2.

get off
the train

3.

get in
the car

4.

get out of
the car

B. 🔊 Listen and repeat.

Let's get off the train.

All right.

C. 🔊 Listen and point below.

D. 🔊 Listen and point. Then sing along.

Phonics Time

A. Make the shape of each letter.

R r   S s

B. 🎧 Listen and point.

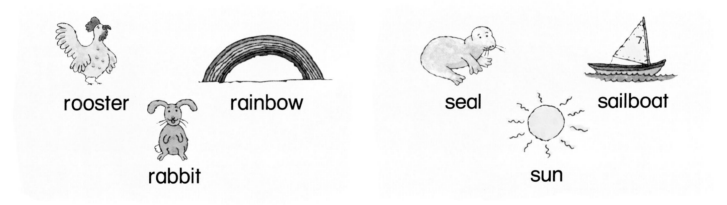

rooster   rainbow   seal   sailboat

rabbit   sun

C. 🎧 Listen and point. Then sing along.

Review 3   Part 1

A. 💿 Listen and match.

1. •   2. •   3. •   4. •   5. •   6. •

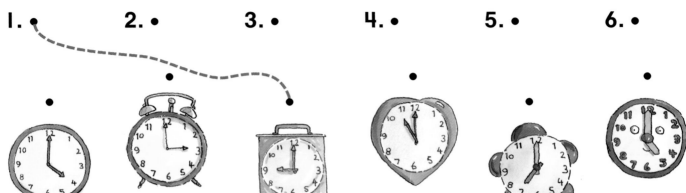

B. 💿 Listen and write the number.

C. Trace the letters. Then circle and connect.

Nn   Oo   Pp   Qq   Rr   Ss

•   •   •   •   •   •

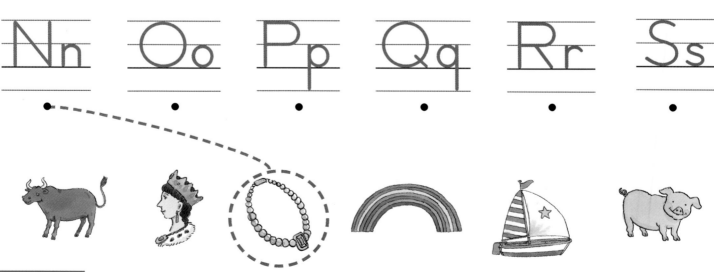

A. 🎧 Listen and connect.

1. •   •  •   •

2. •   •  •   •

3. •   •  •   •

4. •   •  •   •

B. 🎧 Listen and write the number.

Word Time

A. Listen and repeat.

1.  sing songs

2.  write stories

3.  read books

4. color pictures

5.  do jumping jacks

6.  hold hands

B. Listen and point below. Then chant.

C. Listen and write the number.

Use the Words

A. 📼 Listen and repeat.

We read books at school.

B. 📼 Listen and point below.

C. 📼 Listen and point. Then sing along.

Action Word Time

A. 🎵 Listen and repeat.

1.
raise
your hand

2.
put down
your hand

3.
talk to
your friend

4.
listen to
your friend

B. 🎵 Listen and repeat.

Please raise your hand.

Okay.

C. 🎵 Listen and point below.

D. 🎵 Listen and point. Then sing along.

Phonics Time

A. Make the shape of each letter.

B. 🎧 Listen and point.

tiger

table

umbrella

umpire

telephone

upside down

C. 🎧 Listen and point. Then sing along.

A. 🎧 Listen and repeat.

1.  play basketball

2.  play soccer

3. play cards

4.  play chess

5. play the violin

6. play the piano

B. 🎧 Listen and point below. Then chant.

C. 🎧 Listen and write the number.

Use the Words

A. 🎧 Listen and repeat.

Can you play soccer?

Yes, I can.

No, I can't.

B. 🎧 Listen and point below.

C. 🎧 Listen and point. Then sing along.

Action Word Time

A.  Listen and repeat.

1.
bounce the
basketball

2.
catch the
basketball

3.
kick the
soccer ball

4.
throw the
soccer ball

B. Listen and repeat.

I can bounce the basketball.

Great!

C. Listen and point below.

D. Listen and point. Then sing along.

Phonics Time

A. Make the shape of each letter.

V   V   W   W

B. 💿 Listen and point.

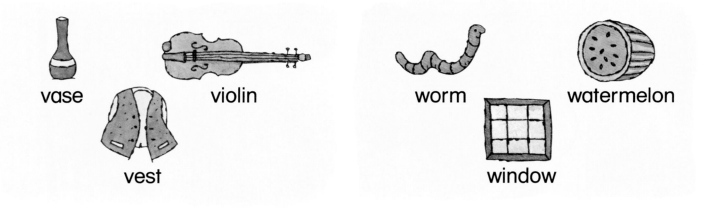

vase   violin   worm   watermelon

vest   window

C. 💿 Listen and point. Then sing along.

Word Time

A. Listen and repeat.

1.  bedroom

2. bathroom

3.  yard

4. living room

5.  dining room

6.  kitchen

B. Listen and point below. Then chant.

C. Listen and write the number.

Use the Words

A. 🎧 Listen and repeat.

B. 🎧 Listen and point below.

C. 🎧 Listen and point. Then sing along.

Action Word Time

A.  Listen and repeat.

1.
wash
the dishes

2.
dry
the dishes

3.
turn on
the light

4.
turn off
the light

B. Listen and repeat.

Turn off the light, please.

All right.

C. Listen and point below.

D. Listen and point. Then sing along.

Phonics Time

A. Make the shape of each letter.

X x Y y Z z

B. 🎧 Listen and point.

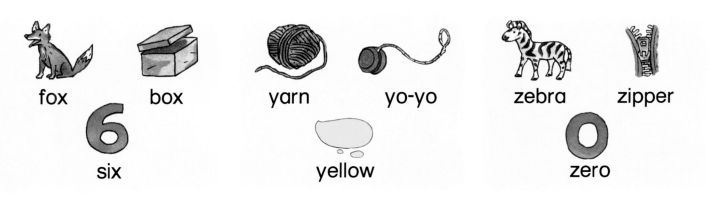

fox   box   yarn   yo-yo   zebra   zipper

six   yellow   zero

C. 🎧 Listen and point. Then sing along.

A. Listen and match.

1.•   2.•   3.•   4.•   5.•   6.•

B. Listen and write the number.

C. Trace the letters. Then circle and connect.

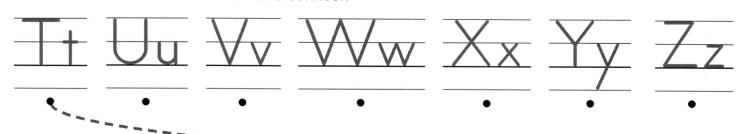

Tt   Uu   Vv   Ww   Xx   Yy   Zz

A. 📼 Listen and connect.

1. •   •  •   •

2. •   •  •   •

3. •   •  •   •

4. •   •  •   •

B. 📼 Listen and write the number.

My Picture Dictionary

Check (✔) the words you know.

A

- [ ] alligator
- [ ] ant
- [ ] apple

- [ ] box
- [ ] bread
- [ ] bus
- [ ] butterfly

B

- [ ] baby
- [ ] ball
- [ ] bathroom
- [ ] bedroom
- [ ] big
- [ ] bounce the basketball

C

- [ ] cake
- [ ] cap
- [ ] car
- [ ] cat
- [ ] catch the basketball
- [ ] climb a tree
- [ ] close the door

☐ cloudy

☐ cold

☐ color pictures

☐ cut the pizza

D

☐ dentist

☐ dining room

☐ dinosaur

☐ do jumping jacks

☐ doctor

☐ doll

☐ donut

☐ draw a picture

☐ dress

☐ drink the juice

☐ dry the dishes

E

☐ eat the pizza

☐ egg

☐ eight o'clock

☐ elephant

☐ eleven o'clock

☐ elf

☐ erase the word

F

- [ ] fan
- [ ] farmer
- [ ] fast
- [ ] feather
- [ ] feed the turtle
- [ ] firefighter
- [ ] five o'clock
- [ ] fly the kite
- [ ] four o'clock
- [ ] fox
- [ ] Friday

G

- [ ] garden
- [ ] get in the car
- [ ] get off the train
- [ ] get on the train
- [ ] get out of the car
- [ ] giraffe
- [ ] girl
- [ ] goat
- [ ] gorilla

H

- [ ] help the teacher
- [ ] hen

☐ hold hands

☐ hold the starfish

☐ horse

☐ hot

☐ house

☐ igloo

☐ ink

☐ insect

☐ jacket

☐ jar

☐ jeans

☐ juice

☐ jump

☐ jump rope

☐ kangaroo

☐ ketchup

☐ key

☐ kick the soccer ball

☐ king

☐ kitchen

☐ kite

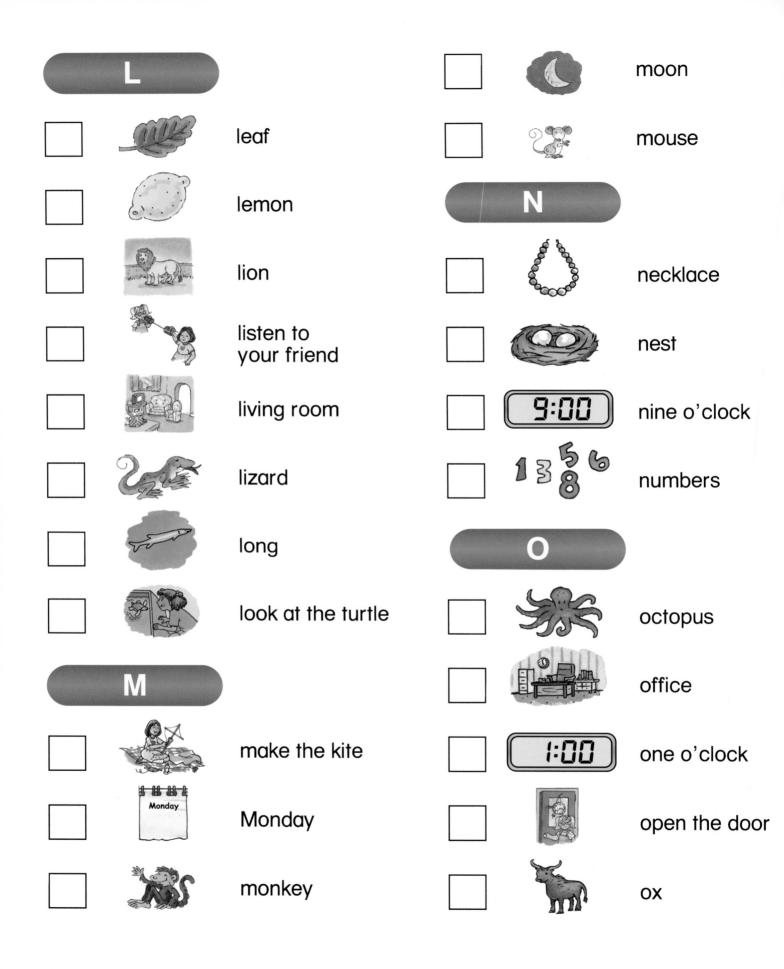

L

- [ ] leaf
- [ ] lemon
- [ ] lion
- [ ] listen to your friend
- [ ] living room
- [ ] lizard
- [ ] long
- [ ] look at the turtle

M

- [ ] make the kite
- [ ] Monday
- [ ] monkey

- [ ] moon
- [ ] mouse

N

- [ ] necklace
- [ ] nest
- [ ] nine o'clock
- [ ] numbers

O

- [ ] octopus
- [ ] office
- [ ] one o'clock
- [ ] open the door
- [ ] ox

☐ paint a picture

☐ penguin

☐ pick up the clock

☐ pig

☐ pilot

☐ pizza

☐ plant a tree

☐ play basketball

☐ play cards

☐ play chess

☐ play soccer

☐ play the piano

☐ play the violin

☐ point to the teacher

☐ polar bear

☐ popcorn

☐ pour the juice

☐ pull the wagon

☐ puppy

☐ push the wagon

☐ put away your sweater

☐ put down the clock

☐ put down your hand

☐ put on your cap

☐ puzzle

☐ queen

☐ question mark

☐ quilt

☐ rabbit

☐ rainbow

☐ rainy

☐ raise your hand

☐ read books

☐ rice

☐ rooster

☐ run

☐ sailboat

☐ salad

☐ Saturday

☐ seal

☐ seven o'clock

☐ shirt

☐ short

☐ sing songs

☐ six

☐ six o'clock

☐ skirt

☐ slow

☐		small
☐		spaghetti
☐		stretch
☐		student
☐		sun
☐		Sunday
☐		sunny
☐		sweater
☐		swim

T

☐		table
☐		take off your cap
☐		take out your sweater

☐		talk to your friend
☐		teacher
☐		telephone
☐	10:00	ten o'clock
☐	3:00	three o'clock
☐		throw the soccer ball
☐		Thursday
☐		tiger
☐		touch the starfish
☐		Tuesday
☐		turn on the light
☐	12:00	twelve o'clock
☐	2:00	two o'clock

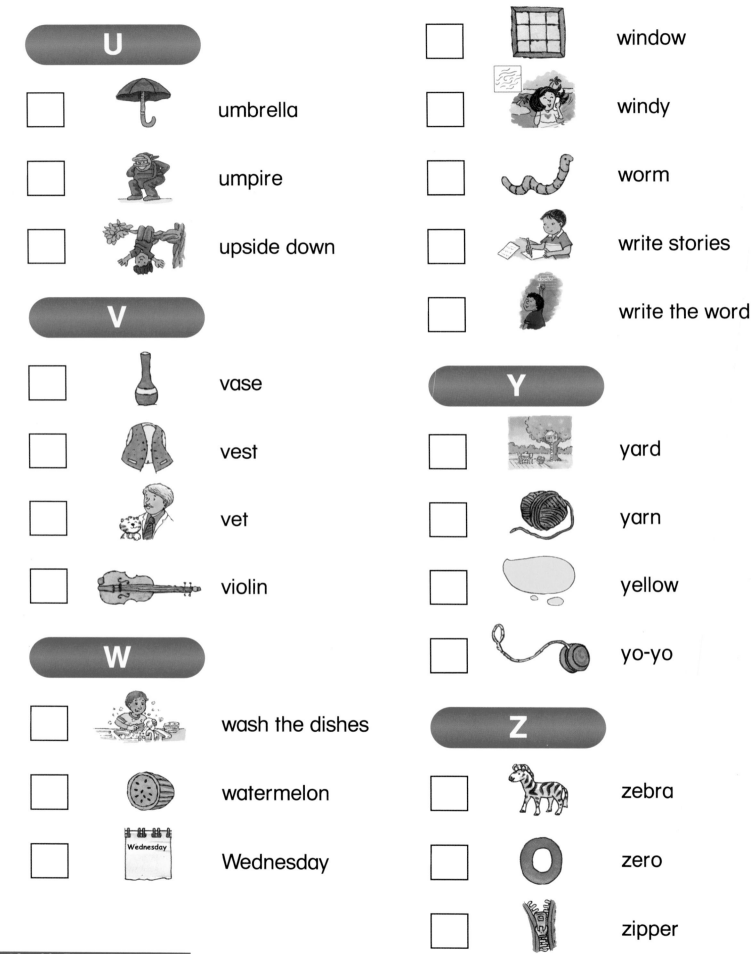

U

☐ umbrella

☐ umpire

☐ upside down

V

☐ vase

☐ vest

☐ vet

☐ violin

W

☐ wash the dishes

☐ watermelon

☐ Wednesday

☐ window

☐ windy

☐ worm

☐ write stories

☐ write the word

Y

☐ yard

☐ yarn

☐ yellow

☐ yo-yo

Z

☐ zebra

☐ zero

☐ zipper

Songs and Chants

Introductions

The Hello Song

Hello! I'm Annie.
Hello, hello, hello!
Hello! I'm Ted.
Hello, hello, hello!
Hello, I'm Digger.
Hello, hello, hello!
Hello, I'm Dot.
Hello, hello, hello!

Hello! I'm Kelly.
Hello, hello, hello!
Hello! I'm Pat.
Hello, hello, hello!
Hello, I'm Kumi.
Hello, hello, hello!
_____
Hello, hello, hello!

Hello, I'm Joe.
Hello, hello, hello!
Hello! I'm Jane.
Hello, hello, hello!
Hello! I'm Chris.
Hello, hello, hello!
_____
Hello, hello, hello!

Unit 1

Word Time

The Kangaroo Chant

Lion, lion, * * kangaroo
Lion, lion, * * kangaroo

Penguin, penguin, * * kangaroo
Penguin, penguin, * * kangaroo

Polar bear, polar bear, * kangaroo
Polar bear, polar bear, * kangaroo

Giraffe, giraffe, * * kangaroo
Giraffe, giraffe, * * kangaroo

Gorilla, gorilla, * * kangaroo
Gorilla, gorilla, * * kangaroo

Kangaroo, kangaroo, * kangaroo
Kangaroo, kangaroo, * kangaroo

Use the Words

The Zoo Song

What is it?
   It's a penguin.
What is it?
   It's a lion.
What is it?
   It's a polar bear.
A penguin, a lion, a polar bear. *

What is it?
   It's a giraffe.
What is it?
   It's a gorilla.
What is it?
   It's a kangaroo.
A giraffe, a gorilla, a kangaroo. *

Action Word Time

I Can Jump

Jump, jump, I can jump.
   Me, too.
Jump, jump, I can jump.
   Me, too.
Jump, jump, I can jump.
   Me, too.
Jump, jump, jump, jump, I can jump!

Run, run, I can run.
   Me, too.
Run, run, I can run.
   Me, too.
Run, run, I can run.
   Me, too.
Run, run, run, run, I can run!

Swim, swim, I can swim.
   Me, too.
Swim, swim, I can swim.
   Me, too.
Swim, swim, I can swim.
   Me, too.
Swim, swim, swim, swim, I can swim!

Stretch, stretch, I can stretch.
   Me, too.
Stretch, stretch, I can stretch.
   Me, too.
Stretch, stretch, I can stretch.
   Me, too.
Stretch, stretch, stretch, stretch,
I can stretch!

Phonics Time

Ant on the Apple

(Melody: *Jimmy Crack Corn*)

Ant on the apple, /a/, /a/, /a/.
Alligator, alligator, /a/, /a/, /a/.
Ant on the apple, /a/, /a/, /a/.
Sing the letter A.

Baby on the bus, /b/, /b/, /b/.
Butterfly, butterfly, /b/, /b/, /b/.
Baby on the bus, /b/, /b/, /b/.
Sing the letter B.

Unit 2

Word Time

Long and Short

Long and short
Long and short
* * * *
Long and short

Big and small
Big and small
* * * *
Big and small

Fast and slow
Fast and slow
* * * *
Fast and slow

Use the Words

It's Long. It Isn't Short.

It's long. It isn't short.
It's big. It isn't small.
It's slow. It isn't fast.
It's long. It's big. It's slow.

It's short. It isn't long.
It's small. It isn't big.
It's fast. It isn't slow.
It's short. It's small. It's fast.

(Repeat)

Action Word Time

Let's Look at the Turtle

(Melody: *The More We Get Together*)

Let's look at the turtle, the turtle,
the turtle.
Let's look at the turtle, the turtle.
   Okay!

Note: The symbol (*) that appears in some of the songs and chants represents handclaps.

Let's feed the turtle, the turtle, the turtle.
Let's feed the turtle, the turtle.
　Okay!

Let's touch the starfish, the starfish,
the starfish.
Let's touch the starfish, the starfish.
　Okay!

Let's hold the starfish, the starfish,
the starfish.
Let's hold the starfish, the starfish.
　Okay!

Phonics Time
Cake on the Car
(Melody: *Jimmy Crack Corn*)

Cake on the car, /c/, /c/, /c/.
Cat, cat, /c/, /c/, /c/.
Cake on the car, /c/, /c/, /c/.
Sing the letter C.

Dentist on the dinosaur, /d/, /d/, /d/.
Donut, donut, /d/, /d/, /d/.
Dentist on the dinosaur, /d/, /d/, /d/.
Sing the letter D.

Unit 3

Word Time
The Occupations Chant
Doctor, doctor, * firefighter
Doctor, doctor, * firefighter
Doctor, doctor, * firefighter
Teacher * and student

Pilot, pilot, * firefighter
Pilot, pilot, * firefighter
Pilot, pilot, * firefighter
Teacher * and student

Vet, vet, * * firefighter
Vet, vet, * * firefighter
Vet, vet, * * firefighter
Teacher * and student

Use the Words
She's a Teacher!
(Melody: *Hallelujah Chorus*)

She's a teacher! She's a teacher!
She's a teacher! She's a teacher!
(clap, clap, stomp, stomp, clap)

She's a pilot! She's a pilot!
She's a pilot! She's a pilot!
(clap, clap, stomp, stomp, clap)

She's a doctor! She's a doctor!
She's a doctor! She's a doctor!
(clap, clap, stomp, stomp, clap)

He's a vet! He's a vet!
He's a vet! He's a vet!
(clap, clap, stomp, stomp, clap)

He's a student! He's a student!
He's a student! He's a student!
(clap, clap, stomp, stomp, clap)

He's a firefighter! He's a firefighter!
He's a firefighter! He's a firefighter!
(clap, clap, stomp, stomp, clap)

Action Word Time
Help the Teacher
(Melody: *Alouette*)

Please...
Help the teacher.
Point to the teacher.
Help the teacher.
　* * Sure.
Help the teacher.
Point to the teacher.
Help.
Point.

Oh-oh-oh-oh, please...
Write the word.
Erase the word.
Write the word.
　* * Sure.
Write the word.
Erase the word.
Write.
Erase.
Oh-oh-oh-oh-oh!

Phonics Time
Elf on the Egg
(Melody: *Jimmy Crack Corn*)

Elf on the egg, /e/, /e/, /e/.
Elephant, elephant, /e/, /e/, /e/.
Elf on the egg, /e/, /e/, /e/.
Sing the letter E.

Farmer on the feather, /f/, /f/, /f/.
Fan, fan, /f/, /f/, /f/.
Farmer on the feather, /f/, /f/, /f/.
Sing the letter F.

Unit 4

Word Time
The Spaghetti Chant
Spaghetti, spaghetti, spaghetti-etti-etti!
Spaghetti, spaghetti, spaghetti-etti-etti!
　Juice, juice.
Spaghetti-etti-etti!
　Bread, bread.
Spaghetti-etti-etti!
　Salad, salad.
Spaghetti-etti-etti!
　Rice, rice.
Spaghetti-etti-etti!
　Pizza, pizza.
Spaghetti-etti-etti!
　Spaghetti, spaghetti.
Spaghetti-etti-etti!

Use the Words
I Want Pizza
(Melody: *Funiculi, Funicula*)

I want pizza. Tra-la-la-la-la.
I want pizza. Tra-la-la-la-la.
I want bread.
I want juice.
I want salad.
I want rice.
I want pizza. Tra-la-la-la-la.

I want spaghetti. Tra-la-la-la-la.
I want spaghetti. Tra-la-la-la-la.
I want bread.
I want juice.
I want salad.
I want rice.
I want spaghetti. Tra-la-la-la-la.

Action Word Time
Cut the Pizza
(Melody: *Tarantella*)

Cut the pizza, cut the pizza, please.
　* All right.
Eat the pizza, eat the pizza, please.
　* All right.

Pour the juice, pour the juice, please.
　* All right.
Drink the juice, drink the juice, please.
　* All right.

(Repeat)

Phonics Time
Girl on the Goat
(Melody: *Jimmy Crack Corn*)

Girl on the goat, /g/, /g/, /g/.
Garden, garden, /g/, /g/, /g/.
Girl on the goat, /g/, /g/, /g/.
Sing the letter G.

Horse in the house, /h/, /h/, /h/.
Hen, hen, /h/, /h/, /h/.
Horse in the house, /h/, /h/, /h/.
Sing the letter H.

Unit 5

Word Time
The Yo-Yo Chant

Yo-yo, puzzle! * * *
Yo-yo, ball! * * *
Yo-yo, jump rope! * * *
Yo-yo, doll! * * *
Yo-yo, kite! * * *
Yo-yo, ball! * * *
Yo-yo, jump rope! * * *
Yo-yo, doll! * * *

Use the Words
I Have a Ball
(Melody: *Three Blind Mice*)

I have a ball.
I have a ball.
I have a doll.
I have a doll.
I have a jump rope.
I have a puzzle.
I have a yo-yo.
I have a kite.

I have a doll.
I have a doll.
I have a ball.
I have a ball.
I have a jump rope.
I have a puzzle.
I have a yo-yo.
I have a kite.

Action Word Time
Watch Me
(Melody: *The Eensy Weensy Spider*)

Watch me push the wagon.
  * Okay.
Watch me pull the wagon.
  * Okay.

Watch me push the wagon.
Watch me pull the wagon.
Watch me push the wagon.
  * Okay.

Watch me make the kite.
  * * Okay.
Watch me fly the kite.
  * * Okay.
Watch me make the kite. *
Watch me fly the kite. *
Watch me make the kite.
  * * Okay.

Phonics Time
Ink on the Igloo
(Melody: *Jimmy Crack Corn*)

Ink on the igloo, /i/, /i/, /i/.
Insect, insect, /i/, /i/, /i.
Ink on the igloo, /i/, /i/, /i/.
Sing the letter I.

Jeans in the jar, /j/, /j/, /j/.
Jacket, jacket, /j/, /j/, /j/.
Jeans in the jar, /j/, /j/, /j/.
Sing the letter J.

Unit 6

Word Time
The Clothing Chant

Shirt and sweater and
skirt and sweater and
dress and sweater and
cap. * *

(Repeat)

Shirt and jacket and
skirt and jacket and
dress and jacket and
cap. * *

(Repeat)

Use the Words
She Has a Shirt
(Melody: *Polly Wolly Doodle*)

She has a shirt. She has a shirt.
She has a shirt, oh yes! * *

She has a skirt. She has a skirt.
She has a skirt, oh yes! * *

He has a cap. He has a cap.
He has a cap, oh yes! * *

He has a jacket. He has a jacket.
He has a jacket, oh yes! * *

She has a dress. She has a dress.
She has a dress, oh yes! * *

He has a sweater. He has a sweater.
He has a sweater, oh yes! * *

Action Word Time
Put On Your Cap

Put on your cap.
Quickly, quickly.
Take off your cap.
Quickly, quickly.

(Repeat)

Take out your sweater
Quickly, quickly.
Put away your sweater
Quickly, quickly.

(Repeat)

(Repeat all)

Phonics Time
Ketchup on the Key
(Melody: *Jimmy Crack Corn*)

Ketchup on the key, /k/, /k/, /k/.
King, king, /k/, /k/, /k/.
Ketchup on the key, /k/, /k/, /k/.
Sing the letter K.

Lizard on the leaf, /l/, /l/, /l/.
Lemon, lemon, /l/, /l/, /l/.
Lizard on the leaf, /l/, /l/, /l/.
Sing the letter L.

Mouse on the moon, /m/, /m/, /m/.
Monkey, monkey, /m/, /m/, /m/.
Mouse on the moon, /m/, /m/, /m/.
Sing the letter M.

Unit 7

Word Time
The Tick-Tock Chant

One o'clock, tick-tock
  One o'clock, tick-tock
Two o'clock, tick-tock
  Two o'clock, tick-tock
Three o'clock, tick-tock
  Three o'clock, tick-tock
Four o'clock, tick-tock
  Four o'clock, tick-tock

Five o'clock, tick-tock
    Five o'clock, tick-tock
Six o'clock, tick-tock
    Six o'clock, tick-tock
Seven o'clock, tick-tock
    Seven o'clock, tick-tock
Eight o'clock, tick-tock
    Eight o'clock, tick-tock

Nine o'clock, tick-tock
    Nine o'clock, tick-tock
Ten o'clock, tick-tock
    Ten o'clock, tick-tock
Eleven o'clock, tick-tock
    Eleven o'clock, tick-tock
Twelve o'clock, tick-tock
    Twelve o'clock, tick-tock

Use the Words
What Time Is It?
What time is it?
It's one o'clock.
Tick-tock. It's two o'clock. * *

What time is it?
It's three o'clock.
Tick-tock. It's four o'clock. * *

What time is it?
It's five o'clock.
Tick-tock. It's six o'clock. * *

What time is it?
It's seven o'clock.
Tick-tock. It's eight o'clock. * *

What time is it?
It's nine o'clock.
Tick-tock. It's ten o'clock. * *

What time is it?
It's eleven o'clock.
Tick-tock. It's twelve o'clock.*

Action Word Time
Open the Door
Open the door slowly.
Close the door slowly.
Open the door slowly.
Close the door, door, door, door, door.
Open the door slowly.
Close the door slowly.
Open and close the door.* *

Pick up the clock slowly.
Put down the clock slowly.
Pick up the clock slowly.
Put down the clock, clock, clock, clock, clock.
Pick up the clock slowly.
Put down the clock slowly.
Pick up and put down the clock.**

Phonics Time
Numbers in the Nest
(Melody: *Jimmy Crack Corn*)

Numbers in the nest, /n/, /n/, /n/.
Necklace, necklace, /n/, /n/, /n/.
Numbers in the nest, /n/, /n/, /n/.
Sing the letter N.

Ox in the office, /o/, /o/, /o/.
Octopus, octopus, /o/, /o/, /o/.
Ox in the office, /o/, /o/, /o/.
Sing the letter O.

Unit 8

Word Time
The Seven-Day Chant
Sunday, Monday,
Tuesday, Wednesday,
Thursday, Friday,
* Saturday.

Sunday, Monday,
Tuesday, Wednesday,
Thursday, Friday,
* Saturday.

(Repeat)

Use the Words
What Day Is It?
(Melody: *For He's a Jolly Good Fellow*)

Today is Sunday.
Today is Sunday.
Today is Sunday.
Tra-la-la-la-la-la.

Today is Monday.
Today is Monday.
Today is Monday.
Tra-la-la-la-la-la.

Today is Tuesday.
Today is Tuesday.
Today is Tuesday.
Tra-la-la-la-la-la.

Today is Wednesday.
Today is Wednesday.
Today is Wednesday.
Tra-la-la-la-la-la.

Today is Thursday.
Today is Thursday.
Today is Thursday.
Tra-la-la-la-la-la.

Today is Friday.
Today is Friday.
Today is Friday.
Tra-la-la-la-la-la.

Today is Saturday.
Today is Saturday.
Today is Saturday.
Tra-la-la-la-la-la.

Action Word Time
Plant a Tree
(Melody: *Shortening Bread*)

Plant a tree, plant a tree.
Plant, plant, plant a tree with me.

Climb a tree, climb a tree.
Climb, climb, climb a tree with me.

Draw a picture, draw a picture.
Draw, draw, draw a picture with me.

Paint a picture, paint a picture.
Paint, paint, paint a picture with me.

(Repeat)

Phonics Time
Puppy in the Popcorn
(Melody: *Jimmy Crack Corn*)

Puppy in the popcorn, /p/, /p/, /p/.
Pig, pig, /p/, /p/, /p/.
Puppy in the popcorn, /p/, /p/, /p/.
Sing the letter P.

Queen on the quilt, /q/, /q/, /q/.
Question mark, question mark,
/q/, /q/, /q/.
Queen on the quilt, /q/, /q/, /q/.
Sing the letter Q.

Unit 9

Word Time
The Weather Chant

Hot, ** sunny *
   Hot, ** sunny *
Cold, ** sunny *
   Cold, ** sunny *
Hot, ** cloudy *
   Hot, ** cloudy *
Cold, ** cloudy *
   Cold, ** cloudy *
Hot, ** windy *
   Hot, ** windy *
Cold, ** windy *
   Cold, ** windy *
Hot, ** rainy *
   Hot, ** rainy *
Cold, ** rainy *
   Cold, ** rainy *

Use the Words
How's the Weather?

How's the weather?
   It's cloudy.
How's the weather?
   It's cold.
How's the weather?
   It's rainy.
How's the weather?
   It's hot.

How's the weather?
   It's sunny.
How's the weather?
   It's hot.
How's the weather?
   It's windy.
How's the weather?
   It's cold.

It's sunny.
It's rainy.
It's windy.
It's cold.

It's sunny.
It's cloudy.
It's windy.
It's hot.

Action Word Time
Let's Get On the Train
(Melody: *Kookaburra*)

Let's get on the train.
   ** All right.
Let's get off the train.
   ** All right.
Get on the train, get off the train.
* ** * **
Let's get in the car.
   ** All right.
Let's get out of the car.
   ** All right.
Get in the car, get out of the car.
  * ** ** **

(Repeat)

Phonics Time
Rooster on the Rainbow
(Melody: *Jimmy Crack Corn*)

Rooster on the rainbow, /r/, /r/, /r/.
Rabbit, rabbit, /r/, /r/, /r/.
Rooster on the rainbow, /r/, /r/, /r/.
Sing the letter R.

Seal in the sailboat, /s/, /s/, /s/.
Sun, sun, /s/, /s/, /s/.
Seal in the sailboat, /s/, /s/, /s/.
Sing the letter S.

Unit 10

Word Time
Write Stories, Read Books

Stories **
Write stories **
Books ***
Read books ***
Pictures **
Color pictures **
Songs ***
Sing songs ***
Jumping jacks *
Do jumping jacks *
Hands ***
Hold hands **

(Repeat)

Use the Words
What We Do at School
(Melody: *Camptown Races*)

We do jumping jacks at school.
** **
We do jumping jacks at school.
* ***
We sing songs at school.
We read books at school.
We do jumping jacks at school.
* ***
We color pictures at school.
** **
We color pictures at school.
* ***
We hold hands at school.
We write stories at school.
We color pictures at school.
* ***

Action Word Time
Talk to Your Friend

Talk to your friend. Talk to your friend.
** Please talk to your friend.
   Okay.

Listen to your friend. Listen to your friend.
** Please listen to your friend.
   Okay.

Raise your hand. Raise your hand.
** Please raise your hand.
   Okay.

Put down your hand. Put down your hand.
* Please put down your hand.
   Okay.

(Repeat)

Phonics Time
Tiger on the Table
(Melody: *Jimmy Crack Corn*)

Tiger on the table, /t/, /t/, /t/.
Telephone, telephone, /t/, /t/, /t/.
Tiger on the table, /t/, /t/, /t/.
Sing the letter T.

Umbrella on the umpire, /u/, /u/, /u/.
Upside down, /u/, /u/, /u/.
Umbrella on the umpire, /u/, /u/, /u/.
Sing the letter U.

Unit 11

Word Time
Play, Play

Play, play, play, play.
Play soccer, play, play, play.
Play cards, play, play, play.
Play basketball, play, play, play.
Play chess, play, play, play.

Play the violin. * * *
Play the piano. * * *
Play the violin. * * *
Play the piano. * * *

Play soccer, play, play, play.
Play cards, play, play, play.
Play basketball, play, play, play.
Play chess, play, play. * *

Use the Words
Yes, I Can

Can you play the violin?
    Yes, I can.
Can you play the violin?
    No, I can't.

Can you play basketball?
    Yes, I can.
Can you play basketball?
    No, I can't.

Can you play soccer?
    Yes, I can.
Can you play soccer?
    No, I can't.

Can you play chess?
    Yes, I can.
Can you play chess?
    No, I can't.

Can you play cards?
    Yes, I can.
Can you play cards?
    No, I can't.

Can you play the piano?
    Yes, I can.
Can you play the piano?
    No, I can't.

Yes, I can!

Action Word Time
I Can Kick the Soccer Ball

(Melody: *The Muffin Man*)

I can kick the soccer ball,
the soccer ball, the soccer ball.
I can kick the soccer ball.
    * * * * Great!

I can bounce the basketball,
the basketball, the basketball.
I can bounce the basketball.
    * * * * Great!

I can throw the soccer ball,
the soccer ball, the soccer ball.
I can throw the soccer ball.
    * * * * Great!

I can catch the basketball,
the basketball, the basketball.
I can catch the basketball.
    * * * * Great!

Phonics Time
Vase on the Violin

(Melody: *Jimmy Crack Corn*)

Vase on the violin, /v/, /v/, /v/.
Vest, vest, /v/, /v/, /v/.
Vase on the violin, /v/, /v/, /v/.
Sing the letter V.

Worm on the watermelon, /w/, /w/, /w/.
Window, window, /w/, /w/, /w/.
Worm on the watermelon, /w/, /w/, /w/.
Sing the letter W.

Unit 12

Word Time
The Rooms Chant

Bathroom, bedroom, * living room
    Bathroom, bedroom, * living room
Kitchen, bedroom, * living room
    Kitchen, bedroom, * living room
Yard, bedroom, * living room
    Yard, bedroom, * living room

Bedroom, bathroom, * dining room
    Bedroom, bathroom, * dining room
Kitchen, bathroom, * dining room
    Kitchen, bathroom, * dining room
Yard, bathroom, * dining room
    Yard, bathroom, * dining room

Use the Words
Where Are You?

(Melody: *Old Dan Tucker*)

Where are you?
    I'm in the living room.
Where are you?
    I'm in the kitchen.
Where are you?
    I'm in the dining room.
Where are you? * *

Where are you?
    I'm in the bathroom.
Where are you?
    I'm in the yard.
Where are you?
    I'm in the bedroom.
Where are you? * *
(Repeat)

Action Word Time
Turn Off the Light

(Melody: *Twinkle, Twinkle, Little Star*)

Turn on the light, please.
    All right.
Wash the dishes, please.
    All right.
Dry the dishes, please.
    All right.
Turn off the light, please.
    All right.
Turn on the light,
Wash the dishes,
Dry the dishes,
Turn off the light.
(Repeat)

Phonics Time
Fox in the Box

(Melody: *Jimmy Crack Corn*)

Fox in the box, /x/, /x/, /x/.
Six, six, /x/, /x/, /x/.
Fox in the box, /x/, /x/, /x/.
Sing the letter X.

Yarn on the yo-yo, /y/, /y/, /y/.
Yellow, yellow, /y/, /y/, /y/.
Yarn on the yo-yo, /y/, /y/, /y/.
Sing the letter Y.

Zebra on the zipper, /z/, /z/, /z/.
Zero, zero, /z/, /z/, /z/.
Zebra on the zipper, /z/, /z/, /z/.
Sing the letter Z.

Word List

A

a	5
all right	20
alligator	7
ant	7
apple	7
are	55
at	10
away	28

B

baby	7
ball	22
basketball	50, 52
bathroom	54
bedroom	54
big	8
books	46
bounce	52
box	57
bread	18
bus	7
butterfly	7

C

cake	11
can	6
can't	51
cap	26
car	11
cards	50
cat	11
catch	52
chess	50
climb	38
clock	34
close	34
cloudy	40
cold	40
color pictures	46
cut	20

D

day	37
dentist	11
dining room	54
dinosaur	11
dishes	56
do jumping jacks	46
doctor	12
doll	22
donut	11
door	34
down	34
draw	38
dress	26
drink	20
dry	56

E

eat	20
egg	15
eight o'clock	32
elephant	15
eleven o'clock	32
elf	15
erase	14

F

fan	15
farmer	15
fast	8
feather	15
feed	10
firefighter	12
five o'clock	32
fly	24
four o'clock	32
fox	57

G

garden	21
get in	42
get off	42
get on	42
get out of	42
giraffe	4
girl	21
goat	21
gorilla	4
great	52

H

hand	48
hands	46
has	27
have	23
he	27
he's	13
help	14
hen	21
hold hands	46
hold	10
horse	21
hot	40
house	21
how's	41

I

I	6
I'm	55
igloo	25
in	42
ink	25
insect	25
is	5
isn't	9

Friday | 36

friend	48

it	5
it's	5

J

jacket	25
jar	25
jeans	25
juice	18
jump rope	22
jump	6
jumping jacks	46

K

kangaroo	4
ketchup	29
key	29
kick	52
king	29
kitchen	54
kite	22

L

leaf	29
lemon	29
let's	10
light	56
lion	4
listen to	48
living room	54
lizard	29
long	8
look at	10

M

make	24
me	6
Monday	36
monkey	29
moon	29
mouse	29

N

necklace	35
nest	35
nine o'clock	32
no	51
numbers	35

O

o'clock	32
octopus	35
of	42
off	28
office	35
okay	10
on	28
one o'clock	32
open	34
out	28
ox	35

P

paint	38
penguin	4
piano	50
pick up	34
picture	38
pig	39
pilot	12
pizza	18
plant	38
play	50
play basketball	50
play cards	50
play chess	50
play soccer	50
play the piano	50
play the violin	50
please	14
point to	14
polar bear	4
popcorn	39
pour	20

pull	24
puppy	39
push	24
put away	28
put down	34
put on	28
puzzle	22

Q

queen	39
question mark	39
quickly	28
quilt	39

R

rabbit	43
rainbow	43
rainy	40
raise	48
read books	46
rice	18
room	54
rooster	43
run	6

S

sailboat	43
salad	18
Saturday	36
school	47
seal	43
seven o'clock	32
she	27
she's	13
shirt	26
short	8
sing songs	46
six o'clock	32
six	57
skirt	26
slow	8
slowly	34

small	8
soccer	50
soccer ball	52
songs	46
spaghetti	18
starfish	10
stories	46
stretch	6
student	12
sun	43
Sunday	36
sunny	40
sure	14
sweater	26
swim	6

T

table	49
take off	28
take out	28
talk	48
teacher	12
telephone	49
ten o'clock	32
the	10
three o'clock	32
throw	52
Thursday	36
tiger	49
time	33
today	37
to	14
too	6
touch	10
train	42
tree	38
Tuesday	36
turn off	56
turn on	56
turtle	10
twelve o'clock	32
two o'clock	32

U

umbrella	49
umpire	49
up	34
upside down	49

V

vase	53
vest	53
vet	12
violin	50, 53

W

watch	24
watermelon	53
we	47
weather	41
Wednesday	36
what	5
where	55
window	53
windy	40
with	38
word	14
worm	53
write	14
write stories	46

Y

yard	54
yarn	57
yellow	57
yes	51
you	51
your	28
yo-yo	22, 57

Z

zebra	57
zero	57
zipper	57